Congratulations on Your
Special Bundle Of Joy

TAPE HERE

From:

To:

First Class
Postage
Required

TAPE HERE

What is a baby?

A baby's a bundle of cute, cuddly fun,
Who drools on your shoulder and makes "number one,"
Throws food, cries all night, and doesn't stay clean,
A sweet little diaper-soiling machine.

You thought you had problems? Well, they've just begun.
You're probably wondering: What have we done?

TAPE HERE

From:

To:

It's a Party!

We're having a party,
We're all so delighted,
Especially me
'Cause you're not invited!

TAPE HERE

TAPE HERE

From:

To:

*First Class
Postage
Required*

For a Special Grandson
on His Birthday

You're Special it's true—
In an odious way,
So you're out of my will,
Effective today!

Happy Birthday, Grandson!

From *Special Moments*,™ published by Ballantine Books.
Copyright © 1984 by Joe Bodólai and Steven Radlauer.

TAPE HERE

From:

To:

Roses are Red, Violets are Blue . . .

TAPE HERE

*I've got the clap
And now so do you!*

Thinking of You...

TAPE HERE

TAPE HERE

From:

To:

First Class
Postage
Required

Wish you would change.

TAPE HERE

From:

To:

First Class
Postage
Required

TAPE HERE

Darling...

I'm coming.
Oh, God, I'm coming!

Stay Sick!

From:

To:

First Class
Postage
Required

When we heard that you were ill,
    Cheers rang out and corks went flying,
In raucous glee we laughed until
    We wet our pants and started crying!

From:

To:

I Told You So!

Gloating

*This card is just to let you know
That I was right—I told you so!
I told you so, I told you so,
I told you so, I told you so,
I told you so, I told you so,
I told you so, I told you so!*

Shell Be Back

TAPE HERE

From:

To:

First Class
Postage
Required

TAPE HERE

Your mother is a *Special Gal,*
As you, her child, well know,
It's sad she was abducted
By Aliens in a UFO.

Our deepest sympathies are with you
in this *Special Time.*

From *Special Moments,*™ published by Ballantine Books.
Copyright © 1984 by Joe Bodolai and Steven Radlauer.

On the Anniversary
of Our Divorce

TAPE HERE

From:

To:

TAPE HERE

*I mark this occasion
with bubbling good cheer,
Of your absence I'm fonder
with each passing year!*

TAPE HERE

From:

To:

First Class
Postage
Required

To a Special Jury Member

Just a cheery little note
To try to influence your vote—
Go right ahead, send me to jail—
But when I'm out I will not fail
To show up at your home address
And of your family make a mess,
So vote "Not Guilty," let me go,
If not...well, you don't want to know.

I deny sending you this card!

Darling...I Tried...

TAPE HERE

From:

To:

First Class
Postage
Required

TAPE HERE

Darling, I'm sorry, I can't get it up,
I'm like a volcano afraid to erupt,
I can't stand my hangups, they torture me so,
Especially those indicated below:

☐ The problem with my boss
☐ The taxes that I owe
☐ The phone call from my ex
☐ My premature hair loss
☐ My fear of what you'll say
☐ My fear of letting go
☐ My constant fear of sex
☐ The lunch I had today

TAPE HERE

*With Deepest Sympathy
on Your Haircut*

TAPE HERE

Comforting wishes in your time of Humiliation.

From *Special Moments,*™ published by Ballantine Books.
Copyright © 1984 by Joe Bodolai and Steven Radlauer.

TAPE HERE

From:

To:

First Class
Postage
Required

TAPE HERE

YOU were fantastic!

Greetings/One-Night Stand

What a night of Bliss!
Let's have one last Kiss!
I loved it when you Came!
I wish I knew your Name!

Congratulations on Your
Screenplay Deal

TAPE HERE

From:

To:

First Class
Postage
Required

TAPE HERE

I heard the news at a Tinseltown sneak
About your boffo, multi-pic deal,
So let's have lunch sometime next week,
We'll schmooze and nosh and kibbitz and spiel.

You're Beautiful! Love Ya!

TAPE HERE

From:

To:

*First Class
Postage
Required*

TAPE HERE

Sorry About the MESS

Apology/Mess

I admit I made a mess.
I'm guilty of a household crime.
I've caused you untold strain and stress.
It seems I do this all the time.

I hate myself.

If You Let Me...

TAPE HERE

From:

To:

First Class
Postage
Required

TAPE HERE

...I'll #@*! your brains out.

A Special Message
to My Secretary

From:

To:

First Class
Postage
Required

I sees it in the way you walks,
I hears it in the way you talks,
I sho' nuff wanna bang your box,
'Cause lawdy, Momma, you be a Fox!

To a Special Bank Teller

TAPE HERE

From:

To:

First Class
Postage
Required

TAPE HERE

A little note to say...

I'm not here for pleasure,
      I'm not here for fun,
I _am_ here on business—
      This is a gun!

So don't make me shoot,
      Don't try nothin' funny,
Don't touch no alarm—
      Just give me the money!

Love and Happy Birthday
to my LATE HUSBAND

TAPE HERE

From:

To:

First Class
Postage
Required

TAPE HERE

To My Reincarnated Spouse...

Today is still a Special Day,
Although you're dead you're not Away,
In Canine form you're with us yet—
You'll always be our Special Pet.

Heel, Honey!

From:

To:

First Class
Postage
Required

Be My 100th Lover

Braggadocio/Sexual

Since the days of my pubescence
I have parked my bold tumescence
In fourscore and nineteen lovers—
  It's no small accomplishment!

So come be my hundredth lover
And I promise you'll discover
That your time with me, though short, will be
  The best you ever spent!

RSVP immediately.

Limit: Once per customer. Offer null where void.

A Special Thought from Your Employer

Severance/Employee

TAPE HERE

From:

To:

First Class
Postage
Required

TAPE HERE

You're late again! Your work is slack!
You carp and whine behind my back!
A two-hour lunch for you is quick,
And once a week you call in sick!
The only thing that you do well
Is make my life a Living Hell!
I've hated you since you were hired,
So hit the road you scum—you're fired!

To a Wonderful Grandmother
on Her Acquittal.

TAPE HERE

From:

To:

First Class
Postage
Required

Grandmothers are special,
Grandmothers are dear,
They aren't meant to go to jail
For six months to a year.

And when confronted with a pack
Of filthy allegations,
They stand their ground and beat the rap,
Like you, Grandma—Congratulations!

TAPE HERE

From:

To:

Announcement/Menses

First Class
Postage
Required

Relax....

TAPE HERE

I got my period.